CORNISH W.

WALKING WITH DOGS BETWEEN TRURO AND FOWEY

LIZ HURLEY

MUDLARK'S PRESS

I

First Edition, 2018

ISBN: 978-0-9932180-5-7

All maps in this publication are reproduced from Ordnance Survey 1:25,000 maps, with the permission of The Controller of Her Majesty's Stationery Office, Crown copyright.

A CIP catalogue record for this book is available from the British Library.

Mudlark's Press
www.lizhurleywrites.com

CONTENTS

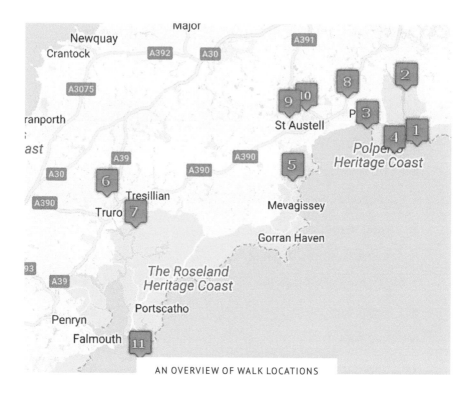

AN OVERVIEW OF WALK LOCATIONS

INTRODUCTION

Welcome to Cornish Walks. This series is designed to help you explore an area in greater depth and will feature a wide range of walks.

Nearly all the walks are circular so you can walk in either direction, although the guide only explains the route one way. If you want a longer walk, just retrace your footsteps for a change of scenery. Some of the shorter walks have a neighbouring walk that they can be linked to. I have said at the start of a walk if this is an option.

At the back of the book, there are some added extras, to enhance your walks. Ranging from recipes and recommended reads to an explanation of how the tides work. I hope that you find them, and the rest of the book, enjoyable.

DOGS

We love walking with our dogs, so I thought I would share some of our absolute favourites with you. We have two Springers, Harry and Agatha, and they like to roam, rummage and generally find every last bit of mud. Because they do like to roam, our favourite walks mainly avoid livestock and cliffs, where these are unavoidable the dogs go back on the lead.

This guide will always let you know when I think a potential hazard is coming up. I haven't bothered mentioning dogs on leads in villages, or on cycle paths or roads. You know what your own dog is capable of; I will only draw your attention to things that you may not know are coming up.

Several of these walks joins cycle paths for a bit, which are likely to also have horse riders on them.

I have also tried to make each walk end near water so that you get a chance to wash them down before they get in the car. You may be lucky enough to have clean dogs, I don't.

All cafés and restaurants mentioned in this book are dog friendly and I have also mentioned where you can find a dog bin.

INSTRUCTIONS

COUNTRY CODE

- Respect the people who live and work in the countryside. Respect private property, farmland and all rural environments.

- Do not interfere with livestock, machinery and crops.

- Respect and, where possible, protect all wildlife, plants and trees.

- When walking, use the approved routes and keep as closely as possible to them.

- Take special care when walking on country roads.

- Leave all gates as you find them and do not interfere with or damage any gates, fences, walls or hedges.

- Guard against all risks of fire, especially near forests.

- Always keep children closely supervised while on a walk.

- Do not walk the Ways in large groups and always maintain a low profile.

- Take all litter home - leaving only footprints behind.

- Keep the number of cars used to the minimum and park carefully to avoid blocking farm gateways or narrow roads.

- Minimise impact on fragile vegetation and soft ground.

- Take heed of warning signs - they are there for your protection.

The Countryside Code states that:
- By law, you must keep your dog under effective control so that it does not disturb or scare farm animals or wildlife. On most areas of open country and common land, known as 'access land' you must keep your dog on a short lead between 1 March and 31 July, and all year round near farm animals.

- You do not have to put your dog on a lead on public paths, as long as it is under close control. But as a general rule, keep your dog on a lead if you cannot rely on its obedience. By law, farmers are entitled to destroy a dog that injures or worries their animals.

- If livestock chase you and your dog, it is safer to let your dog off the lead – don't risk getting hurt by trying to protect it.

- Take particular care that your dog doesn't scare sheep and lambs or wander where it might disturb birds that nest on the ground and other wildlife – eggs and young will soon die without protection from their parents.

- Everyone knows how unpleasant dog mess is and it can cause infections – so always clean up after your dog and get rid of the mess responsibly. Also make sure your dog is wormed regularly to protect it, other animals and people.

- At certain times, dogs may not be allowed on some areas of access land or may need to be kept on a lead. Please follow any signs.

Cattle

- If you find yourself in a field of suddenly wary cattle, move away as carefully and quietly as possible, and if you feel threatened by cattle then let go of your dog's lead and let it run free rather than try to protect it and endanger yourself. The dog will outrun the cows, and it will also outrun you.

- Those without canine companions should follow similar advice: move away calmly, do not panic and make no sudden noises. Chances are the cows will leave you alone once they establish that you pose no threat.

- If you walk through a field of cows and there happen to be calves, think twice; if you can, go another way and avoid crossing fields.

Tides

- There is a useful explanation on tides at the back of the book.

GUIDE TO THE LEGEND

Before heading off for a walk read the description first. You may discover issues with it. Cows, number of stiles, mud etc. Then have a look at a map, not the little one provided with the walk, to get a proper feel for the direction of the walk.

LENGTH: This has been calculated using a range of GPS tracking devices.
EFFORT: Easy to Challenging. These descriptions are only in relation to each other in this book. Every walk has at least one hill in it; not everyone finds hills easy. Challenging, this is for the hardest walks in the book, it will be based on effort and duration. However, nothing in here is particularly tortuous.
TERRAIN: If it's been raining a lot, please assume that footpaths will be muddy. Coast paths tend to be a bit better, near villages they tend to be a bit worse.
FOOTWEAR: I usually walk in walking boots, trainers or ridge sole welling-tons. Except for village walks, smart shoes, sandals, heels or flip flops are unsuitable. Crocs are always unsuitable.*
LIVESTOCK: It is possible that you won't encounter any livestock on a walk that mentions them. Please read the Countryside Code section, on how to avoid them if you do.
PARKING: Postcode for sat nav given. Be aware Cornwall is not always kind to sat navs, have a road map to hand and check you know where you are heading before you set off.
WCs: Due to council cuts, lots of loos are now closed or run by local parishes with seasonal opening hours. If they are an essential part of your walk, check online first. Lots are now coin operated.
CAFÉ / PUB: Local recommendations. Always check ahead, some will have seasonal opening hours.
OS MAP: This will be the largest scale available for the area.
DOG BINS: Almost all of these walks will have at least one dog bin some-where along the route.
BRIEF DESCRIPTION: Just a quick outline of the walk.

DIRECTIONS: If I say, "going up the road" up or down means there is a slope. If I refer to North or SW, you will need a compass. Most smartphones have built-in compasses. It won't be essential as other directions will be given, but it will be an aide. Especially in woodland where there are few other clues.

IN SIZE OF SCALE, LARGEST TO SMALLEST: Road, lane, unmade road, track, trail, path. Although some of the smaller descriptions are interchangeable.

OPTIONS: Several of the walks have options or alternate routes to avoid mud, cattle, seasonal access etc. You only need to choose one option, but please read the whole section first. It will help to rule out any confusion.

THINGS CHANGE: Trees fall down, posts get broken, signs become obscured, footpaths can be closed for repair. Do not be alarmed if you can't see a marker.

TIDES: Occasionally I refer to the fact that a high spring tide might block the path, this tends to only last for about an hour, every few months, in the early morning or evening. You are unlikely to be hindered but it is worth pointing out.

LINKS: In the print book, I have shortened very long hyperlinks for ease of typing and I have left easy hyperlinks as they are. In the e-book they are active.

*JOKE**

**NOT REALLY :D

<u>1</u>

FOWEY HALL WALK

LENGTH: 3.5 miles
EFFORT: Moderate
TERRAIN: Footpath
FOOTWEAR: Trainers, boots
LIVESTOCK: Some potential but alternate route available
PARKING: Caffa Mill car park. PL23 1DF. The walk starts at this point, but you may want to park in the car park on the edge of the village. In August driving to the starting point can be tricky and also very busy
WCs: Fowey
CAFÉ / PUB: Fowey
OS MAP: 107
DOG BINS: Car park

BRIEF DESCRIPTION: A beautiful and popular walk, loved since at least the Tudor times. This version offers a slightly different path, adding a ruined mediaeval chapel, a stunning ancient church and a chance to paddle and maybe spot a seal or two. You even get two boat rides! Dogs are welcomed on the boats.

You do need to pay for the boat taxis, sailings are regular but check their websites, in the links section.

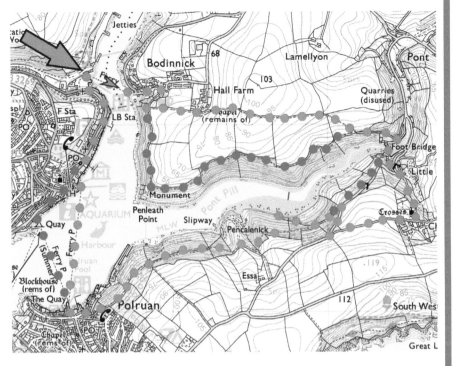

Elevation Profile

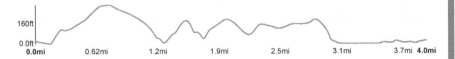

160ft							
0.0ft							
0.0mi	0.62mi	1.2mi	1.9mi	2.5mi	3.1mi	3.7mi	4.0mi

OFF ON AN ADVENTURE

DIRECTIONS:

1. Start at the Caffa Mill car park and take the *ferry* over to Bodinnick, enjoying the *sights from the water.* Stepping off, walk uphill passing the Old Ferry Inn and some large anchors on your left. Continue up past St Johns Church on your right, and just after the Old School House you will see a signpost for the start of the *Hall Walk*, heading towards Pont and Polruan.

2. As you reach the large granite war memorial with a sword engraved on it, you now have two options.

Hall Walk: Originally a promenade for Hall Manor, built just above Bodinnick in the thirteenth century, it was mentioned by Richard Carew in 1585 as *"evenly levelled, to serve for bowling, floored with sand, for soaking up the rayne, closed with two thorne hedges, and banked with sweete senting flowers: It wideneth to a sufficient breadth, for the march of five or six in front, and extendeth, to not much lesse,*

OPTION ONE

To continue along the regular Hall Walk stick to this path. This will take in the *Q Memorial* on Penleath Point with lovely views down the River Fowey, the path is clear, level and mainly wooded. There is no chance of cattle on this route and is great for dogs to have a roam. We re-join Option Two, just above Pont, at Step 6.

OPTION TWO

Chance of cattle and steep hill but open fields, stunning views and a ruined chapel.

3.　Just before the war memorial, take the stile on your left. There is a little gate for dogs as well. The signpost says Pont via Hall Farm, 1 mile. Walk along the left-hand edge of the field heading up to the metal gate in the corner. There may be cattle in these fields and dogs should be on leads. This whole section is well signed with yellow arrows on round discs.

4.　Go through the gate and into a farm drive, walk uphill, just as you clear the farm buildings you will get to the ruined *Hall Chapel* on your left. You are welcome to enter and explore but be aware of all the scaffolding and keep dogs on a short lead.

then halfe a London mile .....and is converted on the foreside, into platformes, for the planting of Ordinance, and the walkers sitting; and on the back part, into Summer houses, for their more private retrait and recreation." It stopped at Penleath Point where the Q Memorial stands. Nowadays, the walk extends around to Polruan.

i Hall Chapel: "The chapel, dedicated to St John the Baptist is recorded in 1374. It belonged to the Mohun family, whose mansion lay to the north and was also probably used for public worship. The antiquarians of the 19th century recorded its subsequent re-use as a barn and granary. Henderson made a full record of it in 1924 and noted that during the conversion the east window had been removed and this wall rebuilt to accommodate the cart doorway and a second storey loft had been inserted. He also noted the oak cradle roof was almost perfect and said an enclosure to the south had contained a cemetery." Historic England.

5.　Return to the concrete drive and continue uphill. At the top the drive ends at three fields. The views to your right are spectacular. Now head into the middle field and walk along the left-hand edge, keep an eye out for the yellow arrows. Through another metal gate and continue along the left-hand edge. From up here, you can see *Lanteglos Church* tower to your right.

6.　Just as you get to the next metal gate there is a lovely example of vertical slate hedging and a sheep *stile*. Go through the gate and now head diagonally downhill across the field towards the woods. Head toward a tree stump in the middle of the field and beyond it in the corner of the field is the next gate and coffen stile. This is where we rejoin Option One.

7.　Go through the wooden gate and follow the path left, downhill to *Pont* you can catch glimpses below on your right. At the T-junction, the signpost says Polruan, take this, turning right and heading down into Pont. Walk across the river and head forwards passing the large buildings, keeping an eye out for a wooden National Trust signpost at knee level pointing the way. Walk past Pont Creek Cottage and take the obvious path uphill with the stream on your left.

Pont and Pont Creek:
Pont Creek is also known as Pont Pill. Pill being derived from the Cornish word, pyll, meaning creek. Many of the smaller creeks are called pills. Pont is an old word for ferryboat, usually a chain boat. It's also French for bridge. Both origins of the word seem appropriate. The large buildings on either side of the river are lime kilns and until the last century, this was a busy little quay. Pont Creek itself is a great place to sit and spot wildlife including the odd seal.

8. Continue up the path to *Lanteglos Church*, ignoring the right-hand path to Polruan. It's 370 yards uphill, but it really is a special church, I've never seen so much original woodwork inside a parish church. If this doesn't appeal, take the right-hand path to Polruan. Halfway up the path to the church, it crosses a small road, head over and continue up, with the stream again on your left. There is a water bowl at the front door of the church for dogs.

9. Having explored the church and graveyard head out onto the road in front, and walk right. This is a very quiet country lane and is festooned with flowers in spring and summer. At the T-junction turn right and walk downhill, after a short while there is a wooden gate on your left. Go through the gate and turn left onto the footpath, which immediately splits. Take the right-hand fork heading downhill, it is signed Polruan 1¼ mile. This is where we rejoin the Hall Walk, continue with the river below on your right. It is now fine to let your dog off the lead.

10. For another pleasant diversion, you can take the next right-hand footpath down to *Pont Creek* for a chance to paddle and keep an eye out for seals in the river. When you are ready to continue, carry along the path uphill, this return path is quite steep, but there is a bench at the top, should you feel the need for a quick moment of contemplation.

i **Lanteglos Church:** Legend has it that St Wyllow was beheaded for reasons unknown. Unhappy with his predicament he picked up his head, walked half a mile and placed it down by a bridge, indicating that this was to be his final resting place. Lanteglos Church was then built on that spot. This is a grade one listed church with evidence of Norman features in its tower arches and doorway. Everywhere you look are unusual features, from the very ornate and unusual stone cross with a lantern head, to the wooden wagon roof and painted wooden panelling.

LANTEGLOS CHURCH

11. Turn right and continue along on the main Hall Walk. Just after the bench, the path crosses a small lane. This is a very quiet lane but you may want to get your dog back on its lead, just whilst you cross over. Continue along the path keeping an eye out for a *pillbox* on your left just before another bench. You are now above Polruan. As you head down into the village, you walk down a flight of steps, then turn right and head down another flight, keep heading down until you get to the quay. The ferry leaves from the slipway by the public loos.

12. The ferry either goes to the Whitehouse Pier or the Town Quay, whichever one you get on when you disembark turn right and follow the road through the town, it will be a slightly longer walk if you get dropped off at Whitehouse Pier. There are great sights from the river. Follow the main road out of Fowey, walking along the river until you get back to the Caffa Mill car park or wherever you started your walk.

Pillbox: The Polruan pillbox is of the FW3/22 variety, hexagonal in shape, and was built for the Second World War. "A Pillbox is a simple structure made of concrete used to protect and shelter soldiers and machine gun crews from incoming bullets, shrapnel, and shell splinters; while allowing them to return fire." Homefront Legacy.

Sights from the water: As you head out on the Bodinnick ferry, to your left you can see Fowey's deep water docks, massive cruise liners can sometimes be seen in the water as well as giant tankers. These make for a very dramatic sight as they tower above the buildings below. Ahead of you, the blue and white building is Ferryside, once Daphne du Maurier's home.

Heading back across the water from Polruan you can see, to your far left, Henry VIII's naval defences at St Catherine's Castle, then a large crenellated house Point Neptune, built for William Rashleigh in 1862. Looking toward the centre of the village

FERRYSIDE HOUSE

HIDDEN PASSAGES

you can see Fowey Church, the start and end of the Saints Way. Beside it stands the impressive crenellated Place House, built in the fifteenth century and home to the Treffrys a powerful family and large landowners.

LINKS:

Bodinnick Ferry http://www.ctomsandson.co.uk/bodinnick-ferry/
Hall Chapel http://bit.ly/2GilQfc
Pillboxes http://bit.ly/2u69yBK
Polruan Ferry http://www.ctomsandson.co.uk/polruan-ferry/
Q Memorial http://www.quillercouch.co.uk/q-and-fowey-2/
Types of Stiles http://www.cornishhedges.co.uk/PDF/stiles.pdf

PHOTO ALBUM:

https://flic.kr/s/aHsm7etvP9

2

ETHY WOODS

LENGTH: 2.5 miles
EFFORT: Easy
TERRAIN: Riverside footpath
FOOTWEAR: Walking boots in winter, otherwise trainers / shoes
LIVESTOCK: None
PARKING: Lerryn car park. PL22 0PT
WCs: Lerryn
CAFÉ / PUB: The Ship Inn, Lerryn
OS MAP: 107
DOG BINS: At the start of the walk

BRIEF DESCRIPTION: An easy riverside walk through Ethy Woods. Plenty of opportunity to run and splash about, whether two or four legged.

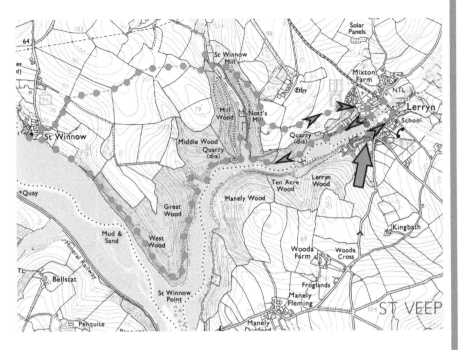

Elevation Profile

200ft								

0.0mi   0.62mi   1.2mi   1.9mi   2.5mi   3.1mi   3.7mi   4.4mi   4.9mi

200ft 130ft 66ft 0.0ft

ETHY MILL

DIRECTIONS:

1. From the *Lerryn* car park, if the stepping stones are visible, cross the river here. If not, then exit the car park onto the road, turn left, walk along the road and head over the bridge. Shortly after the bridge take the first turning on your left, walk to the end and at the T-junction turn left towards the river. You are now looking over to your car park.

Lerryn: The first written evidence of the existence of the village of Lerryn is in the Assize Roll of 1284. The name probably comes from the Cornish word 'lerion' meaning waters. In 1573 Queen Elizabeth I ordered that a rate be levied for rebuilding the bridge in order to aid production of silver.

2.   Turn right and walk along the river. At first, this is a tarmacked road, but gradually the surface deteriorates as the houses thin out until you get to the entrance to the National Trust Ethy Woods. The woodland path hugs the river for about two and a half miles until it gets to St Winnow. It's very clearly laid out and whilst it can be muddy at times it is mostly easy underfoot.

3.   The first section of this river path towards the tiny hamlet of St Winnow is nice and easy. You will pass a mediaeval stone pillar and down to the left of it is the remains of an old quay with stone steps leading into the water. This won't be visible at high tide. Follow the path right and then cross over the creek, do not take the uphill, inland path.

i **King Morholt:** King Morholt was an Irish king, and Uncle to Iseult, demanding a tribute from King Mark, Morholt wanted every boy and girl aged 15, to be given to him to take to Ireland. Tristan was having none of this and challenged King Morholt on behalf of his Uncle. The battle took place on a sandbank island between Lantyan and St Winnow where Tristan successfully slew the King but not before Morholt cut him with a poisoned blade. Tristan was close to death and, with much grieving, King Mark and all his subjects put the hero, Tristan, in a boat and pushed him out to sea. Tristan's boat floated to sea where he was found by Irish fishermen. No one knew who he was and so he was given to Iseult to heal. Thus she fell in love with Tristan not knowing he was her Uncle's killer and her future husband's nephew.

CELTIC CROSSES IN ST WINNOW CHURCH YARD

THE RIVER FOWEY

4.   Carry along the path, across another creek and soon the path will join an unmade road. Walk along the road, after a while, there is a clear turning off to the left. This is a narrow footpath that continues for about a half-mile before rejoining the unmade road. It is closer to the river and more atmospheric but not as easy to walk. Choose either path.

5.   Keep left, following the river until the path ends at a stile. Over the stile and walk along the field keeping the hedge on your left side, over another stile and continue to walk forwards. At the next corner, cross the stile and a small wooden bridge. You are now on the creekside, walk along the edge until you get to the slip-way. During *high tide*, you might get wet feet, and during a very high tide, it might be impassable. Check ahead. Across the river lies Lantyan and on the sandbanks between these two points, the legendary Tristan killed *King Morholt*.

6.   Now turn around and retrace you steps back to the car park.

LINKS:

Lerryn http://lerrynhistory.co.uk/index.cfm
Tide Timetables https://bit.ly/2IOJw9I

PHOTO ALBUM:

https://flic.kr/s/aHsmfP4tkB

3

THREE BEACHES

LENGTH: 4 miles
EFFORT: Easy
TERRAIN: Coast path, beach
FOOTWEAR: Any; footpath can require wellies in winter
LIVESTOCK: None
PARKING: Par Beach car park. PL24 2AR. Free in winter
WCs: Second car park on Par Beach
CAFÉ / PUB: Milo's on Par Beach or The Ship Inn
OS MAP: 107
DOG BINS: Lots in the Par Beach area

BRIEF DESCRIPTION: A good wildlife and beach walk, combining three beaches and the coast path. Due to the varied habitats, this is a great walk for *wildlife* spotting, so pack your binoculars. During the summer, dogs are banned on the Polkerris Beach, although welcomed in all the beer gardens. Par Beach is the most popular dog walking beach in the area and all facilities are dog friendly.

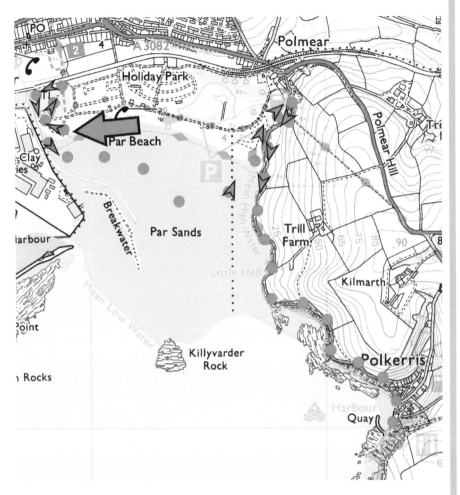

Elevation Profile

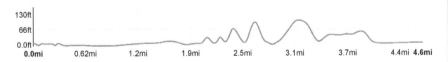

130ft								
66ft								
0.0ft								
0.0mi	0.62mi	1.2mi	1.9mi	2.5mi	3.1mi	3.7mi	4.4mi	4.6mi

DIRECTIONS:

1. From the main road, A3082, turn into Par Sands. Follow the site road all the way to the very far end of the park, the road ends at a small car park. If the site is busy, park in the very large car park that is to the left of the site road just after you leave the main road. If you park in the large car park, start your walk at Step 7 on the instructions and then once you get to Step 9, head straight onto Steps 1, 2, 3 etc.

2. From the small car park take the clear trail that veers to the right, away from the sea, there is a sea safety board beside it. This trail wanders through a

Wildlife: This walk passes water meadows, pine woods, rivers, dunes, ponds, reed beds, cliffs, woodlands, fields and the sea. The variety of birdlife is therefore very impressive, and we are also lucky enough to have interesting visitors, in winter this area has also been home to bitterns. Out to sea, keep your eyes open for seals, dolphins and, in summer, basking sharks. Otters are also rumoured to be in the area, but they are very elusive.

PAR BEACH

wildlife area, stick to the path. Ignore the first clear left-hand turn that leads to the river, walk on and take the next left-hand turn that leads into the woods. It is marked by a large granite boulder with an arrow on it. Follow the path into the pine woods and continue along as it veers left. Eventually, it will loop back to the path you were just on. Turn right, then right again. Now take the right-hand turning towards the river that you ignored earlier and walk down to the water's edge. On the other side of the river, the view is dominated by *Par Docks*.

3.   Walk left along the river bank until you get to the beach. If the *tide* is too high, head back to your car and walk onto the beach from there.

4.   Walk the entire length of the beach. This is the area's most popular dog beach so you are bound to meet other dogs. When you get to the other end turn left and follow the footpath by the stream as it leads into a very large car park. Pop the dog lead on if the car park is busy. Keep following the stream until you get to a small bridge. You should see a sign for the coast path. Cross the bridge, climb a flight of steps and walk up along the coast path. Although there is only one sharp drop on this section it is best to keep your dog on a lead if you think they are prone to bolting.

ROOM TO RUN, JUMP AND SWIM

Par Docks: Par Docks has long dominated the landscape, just as the *china clay industry* dominated every aspect of life in this area of Cornwall. It used to be said that if all four chimneys were blowing that they were making money, if only one chimney was blowing they were running at a loss. I don't know if I've ever seen all four blowing, but they may have improved the refining process. It is, however, a declining industry and soon the docks may close altogether.

5.   When the path takes a sharp left turn uphill, you can take the turning that branches off here, down to Boolies Beach. Boolies is a gorgeous beach and often quiet, as it takes a bit of walking to get to it. This might be considered a good time to turn around, but the walk on to Polkerris is lovely. However, the coast path passes a very steep hidden drop and I always keep my dogs on their leads for this section.

HEADING DOWN TO BOOLIES

6.   Returning to the coast path, head uphill, this section of the path can get close to the cliff edge so best to keep dogs on leads. The path is quite steep, but the views over St Austell Bay are fabulous. Follow the path into woodland and make your way down the hill into *Polkerris*. This is a tiny hamlet with a great pub, restaurant, seasonal café and watersports centre. A dog ban is strictly enforced on the beach between Easter and October, but you can sit, with your dog, in any of the three establishments' courtyards overlooking the beach. Polkerris is very popular in summer and can be very crowded at high tide. It is really lovely though and worth a visit.

7.   Return back the way you came heading along the coast path until you take the flight of steps down into the very large car park at Par Sands.

8. Now walk across the car park and follow the campsite road as it goes past the duck pond. There are lots of wild birds walking about here, so your dogs will need to be on a close lead. Just past the pond is Milo's, a friendly Italian beach café and restaurant.

9. On the other side of the road from the café is a path that leads directly into the sand dunes. Take this path and then take the right-hand turning. There are lots of ways through the dunes, but so long as you keep on a straight path with the road to your right and the sea to your left, you will be fine. Keep walking until the path finishes at the end of the dune system and you should find yourself back by your car.

Polkerris: There are a few places in Cornwall where almost an entire village is owned by one person. Polkerris is one of these places and is owned by the Rashleigh Estate. Its curving harbour wall once supported a thriving fishing industry as well as Napoleonic gun emplacements. It is an idyllic and popular spot and usually avoids the worst of the weather. However, very occasionally in certain conditions, the cove turns into a cauldron.

LINKS:

China Clay Industry https://bit.ly/2G16OGA
Par Beach http://www.parbeach.com/
Par Docks https://bit.ly/2G2GMnf
Polkerris Cauldron 1825 https://bit.ly/2pzRV8K
Polkerris Cauldron - 2012 https://bit.ly/2HVPwvO
Tide Timetables https://bit.ly/2lOJw9l
Wildlife at Par http://www.parbeach.com/wildlife.html

PHOTO ALBUM:

https://flic.kr/s/aHsmbfgE9U

4

LANKELLY LOOP

LENGTH: 2.5 miles
EFFORT: Moderate
TERRAIN: Fields and coast path
FOOTWEAR: Trainers. Boots when muddy. This
is a very popular route and can become quite
churned up after heavy rain
LIVESTOCK: Cattle sometimes on the coast path
PARKING: National Trust Coombe Farm car park.
PL23 1HW. It is possible to join this walk from
Fowey, have a look at the map
WCs: None
CAFÉ / PUB: None
OS MAP: 107
DOG BINS: In the National Trust car park

BRIEF DESCRIPTION: An enjoyable, short walk,
good for dogs with great sea views. There is
the opportunity to explore a small Tudor castle
and visit the sites that were the inspiration for
Rebecca by Daphne du Maurier.

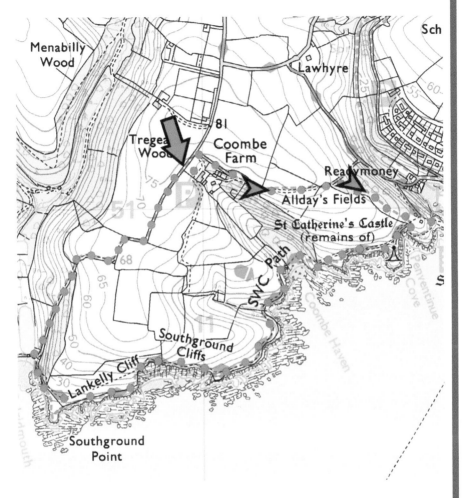

Elevation Profile

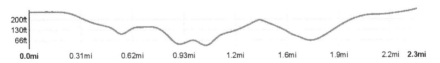

LOOKING BACK TOWARDS FOWEY'S DEEP HARBOUR

DIRECTIONS:

1. From the National Trust Coombe Farm car park, head back towards the road and take the footpath to Coombe Haven. There is a clear fingerpost, pointing the way. At the end of the lane go through the five-bar gate and into a field. Walk across the field taking the more distinctive path veering left. Walk into the second field and then turn left towards the trees and a black, metal kissing gate.

2. Go through the gate and into the woods. After about 10 yards take the smaller path on the right and follow it

St Catherine's Castle: Built in 1538 by Henry VIII to protect Fowey from the threat of a French invasion, it was later modified to house two guns during the Crimean War, and later again, more guns were installed during the Second World War. There is no evidence that the castle defences were ever actually deployed in combat.

down through the woods. It levels out for a bit and then turns left and downhill again, where it stops at the foundations of an old building. Take the steps to the left and head down to a larger footpath. Turn right onto this path and walk towards the English Heritage signpost for *St Catherine's Castle*.

Explore the castle, making sure your dog is on a short lead as there are lots of steep drops, and then return to the English Heritage signpost.

3.   Turn right, back the way you came, and then turn left and immediately turn sharp left and climb a small, steep path up towards the *Rashleigh Mausoleum*. After you have had a look around, head back down to the path, then turn left and walk up to a wooden gate. You are now on the coast path and will stick to this for the next mile.

4.   In the distance is a large red and white tower, this is the Gribben Daymark. We are walking towards it but won't actually walk to it. Dogs can happily roam along this section, but after you pass Coombe Haven, you will go through a gate warning about cattle. The next three fields might have cattle in them, so dogs on leads until you are certain. The coast path also runs close to cliffs so again, dogs on leads. In the third field, it is easy to see if there are any cattle and the path

The Rashleigh Family: This section of Cornwall is utterly dominated by the Rashleigh Estate. Whether it's Point Neptune, the Mausoleum, Gribben Daymark, the village of Polkerris, Charlestown Docks (just beyond this walk), Menabilly, the Rashleigh Inn, or the Waymarker Crosses; the Rashleighs have built it, owned it or developed it. The family rose to power and riches in the Tudor period, settled in the Fowey area, and were no doubt instrumental in the sacking and reallocation of the Tywardreath Priory wealth. They grew their wealth in shipping and mining, and by 1873 Jonathan Rashleigh was the largest landowner in Cornwall.

heads inland, away from the cliffs and towards the woods.

5.   The path now heads into the trees and sharply downhill to Polridmouth Beach. As you walk down, you can see a house sitting by a large ornamental lake. This was the inspiration for the boathouse in Rebecca by Daphne du Maurier.

6.   As you reach the beach take the right-hand footpath heading uphill. This section is long and steep, but when you get to the top, you can enjoy the views back down to the sea. Go through the gate and turn right. Follow along the right-hand edge of the field, turn left at the corner of the field and head towards the wooden gate. Pass through the gate, onto the track and follow it until you return to your car park.

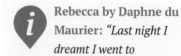 Rebecca by Daphne du Maurier: *"Last night I dreamt I went to Manderley again."* Hidden in the woods, behind the ornamental lake stands Menabilly House, the Rashleigh ancestral home, that serves as the inspiration for Manderley in *Rebecca*. When du Maurier first discovered the house, it was neglected and probably most resembled the wreck that it becomes in her book. *Rebecca* is a sinister, dark novel but it is also a paean to a house. Happily, a few years later she was able to lease Menabilly from the Rashleigh family, restoring it to its former glory, and lived there for twenty-six years.

CRYSTAL CLEAR WATERS

ONCOMING STORM

LINKS:

Daphne du Maurier https://bit.ly/2DQdsyq
Rashleigh Mausoleum https://bit.ly/2BUN2in
St Catherine's Castle https://bit.ly/2G31gMM

PHOTO ALBUM:

https://flic.kr/s/aHskwdbi5G

5

KING'S WOOD

LENGTH: 4 miles
EFFORT: One long hill. The rest is easy
TERRAIN: Woodland, cycle path. Often muddy
FOOTWEAR: Walking boots. In dry weather trainers, etc. should be fine
LIVESTOCK: None
PARKING: King's Wood. PL26 6DJ. This is the closest postcode but it is not exact, look out for the large lay-by and turn in
WCs: Pentewan
CAFÉ / PUB: Pentewan
OS MAP: 105
DOG BINS: Several along the route

BRIEF DESCRIPTION: A sheltered woodland and river stroll, once away from the cycle trails the dogs can have fun roaming through the trees. Let's give the squirrels some exercise.

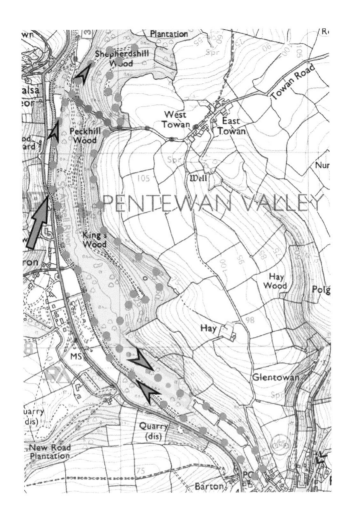

Elevation Profile

0.0mi	0.62mi	1.2mi	1.9mi	2.5mi	3.1mi	3.7mi	4.0mi

260ft
200ft
130ft
66ft

OLD TRACKWAYS

DIRECTIONS:

1. From the car park (not the lay-by), looking towards the main road, take the right-hand path and walk upstream, along the river. Follow this path in through *King's Woods* and over a small bridge until it joins a larger unmade road. Turn right and head up into a parking area /clearing. For this first section, you may want to keep your dog on a lead if they aren't good with bikes. Equally the path crosses a small road.

2. From this second car park area, you now have a choice of two paths that rejoin each other after a short while.

King's Wood: At one point in its history, the woodland was thought to be a designated deer park. If you look at the very fine retaining wall at the very highest point of the walk, you will see that it was constructed with over-capped stones, presumably to stop deer leaping out.

34

OPTION ONE

This is a lovely meandering stroll up through the woods with plenty of space for your dogs to run.

Within the parking area, there are three exits. Go through the kissing gate by the five-bar gate to the left of the car park. Follow the path uphill, after about five minutes it turns sharply to the right, almost back on itself. It is still the principle path so ignore any other left or right-hand turns. This path ends at a large open clearing with several exits. You are heading for the top left exit by the bench after which the path goes uphill into the wood.

Follow the path as it dips down to the right, up again and then heads downhill, veering left through the pine trees. At the edge of a steep ridge looking down, the path becomes difficult to see. You need to be walking on a compass bearing of around 150 degrees SSE.

There are some steps cut into the hillside, and they swing around to 210 degrees SSW. Keep heading SW, and the final few steps will end at a Woodland Trust post. The path then meets the old road mentioned in Option Two. Turn left and walk uphill for a few metres until you see the path off to the right of the road, marked by another Woodland Trust post.

White River / St Austell River: The valley floor of this river was used for tin streaming, a way to catch tin deposits floating downstream, this practice would turn the water red. In more recent centuries the river changed colour from red to white. As china clay was extensively mined in the St Austell region, the whole area including the rivers turned white as they carried the run-off. In heavy rain, the sea itself would turn white where a river ran into it. Even today, in very heavy rain the river will turn a milky colour.

Pentewan: Pentewan was first mentioned in 1086 in the Domesday Book and has continued as a small working village across the years. It has benefited from having a local quarry extracting Pentewan Stone, having tin extracted from the local river, being a major port for the china clay industry with a railway line serving it from St Austell, and finally, from being a home for fishing boats and the pilchard industry. If you choose to walk around the village you will see many remnants of its long industrial heritage.

If you lost the path coming down through the trees, you will need to re-navigate yourself up or down the old road accordingly, until you find the Woodland Trust post.

OPTION TWO

A short, sharp climb uphill.

To the left and right of the parking area are two five-bar gates, in between, and in front of you is the continuation of the old road. It is very atmospheric but also very steep. Towards the top of the hill and just before the road turns sharply to the left, you turn right at the Woodland Trust post, leaving the old road and onto a woodland path.

This is where the two options rejoin.

3.	Stepping off the old road by the Woodland Trust post, turn left uphill towards the skyline, following the intermittent steps. You should now be walking in a SW direction with a stone wall to your left and fields beyond the wall. Follow this path for about a mile. After roughly three-quarters of a mile, and just after a bench, the path turns right and begins to head steeply downhill. It zigs once, sharp right and then zags sharp left at another Woodland Trust post. The path now veers right but splits into two at the tree with a red fairy door at the base of its trunk. Take the left-hand path and continue downhill.

Pentewan is well worth a visit and has a great pub, café, loos and beach. Little Bay Café offer free water refills and are very dog-friendly. Their location is in the links section at the end of this walk. They are just by the pub.

KING'S WOOD

4.   This path heads over a stream bed, shortly after, on your right, is the remnants of a woodlander's cottage. The path turns right and continues downhill until it opens into another large grass clearing. From here you now need to take the path off to the left, marked by another post. Head back into the wood and downhill, as the path levels out it turns left towards a small wooden bridge that crosses a stream.

5.   Head over the footbridge and bear right, through the beech and oak trees. Keep any posts you see to your right and head down to your left towards a stream and a series of causeways. This section of the valley floor is often very wet and/or muddy. The path through is clear until the second to last causeway when it seems to stop, the final causeway is about 70 steps away in a SW direction. You may need to weave about a bit to find a non-muddy section.

6.   Once on the causeway, walk towards the edge of the wood. You now pop out onto the cycle path alongside the *White River*.

7.   From here on the navigation is easy. Turn left and follow the river, downstream, after about a hundred yards the cycle path turns left, back into the woods. Stay on this path for about half a mile until just after a dog bin, and just before you reach the Cycle Hire Centre at *Pentewan*. This walk doesn't go into the village but it is worth an exploration if you have the time.

8.   Continuing the walk, return to this point. There is now a right-hand turning by the dog bin. Take this path to the river's edge and turn right. You now walk upstream all the way back to your car, roughly a mile away.

LINKS:

Kings Wood https://bit.ly/2pKiDvA
Little Bay Café https://bit.ly/2IdsUHh
Tin Streaming https://bit.ly/2GeJUAs

PHOTO ALBUM:

https://flic.kr/s/aHsm4pNywk

CAN BE MUDDY!

6

IDLESS GUNPOWDER WALK

LENGTH: 3 miles. Option to shorten at two points
EFFORT: Easy to moderate
TERRAIN: Good footpaths
FOOTWEAR: Trainers or boots
LIVESTOCK: None
PARKING: TR4 9QT. Idless Forestry Commission car park
WCs: None
CAFÉ / PUB: Woodman's Cabin. They also have a little dog shower for muddy feet
OS MAP: 105
DOG BINS: In the car park

BRIEF DESCRIPTION: A short and enjoyable walk, there is the option to shorten it by a mile. You are bound to spot buzzards flying overhead as they look down on you exploring an ancient hillfort and gunpowder stores. There may be cyclists, but this is not a cycle network and there are no cliffs or livestock, making this a lovely walk for dogs to be off lead for the entire walk.

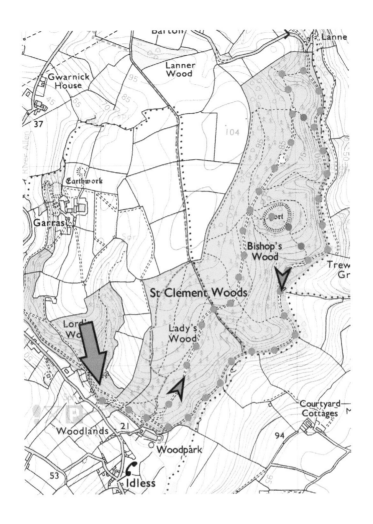

Elevation Profile

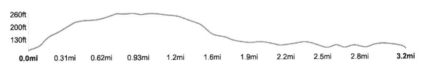

260ft									
200ft									
130ft									
0.0mi	0.31mi	0.62mi	0.93mi	1.2mi	1.6mi	1.9mi	2.2mi	2.5mi	2.8mi	**3.2mi**

DIRECTIONS:

1. From the car park take the wide unmade road uphill.

Head uphill for just under a mile, carry on past a bench and some footpath signs, and keep walking until the path starts to level out. Now start to look ahead and to your right and you will hopefully notice a large clump of trees that look different to all the other trees in the area. They are deciduous rather than coniferous and in a very obvious group. These trees mark the location of the *hillfort*. Keep walking until you are almost level with them and you will see three paths, all close to each other, to the right of the trail.

2. Take the middle path which will take you straight into the heart of the hillfort. If you find yourself bypassing the fort you have picked the wrong path. Stick to the path walking through the fort and you can clearly see the defensive ramparts and ditches.

If you wish to do the shorter walk, stay on this path as it heads downhill to the valley floor. You will rejoin the main walk at Step 6. Once on the valley floor turn left to explore the *Gunpowder Works*.

Hillfort: This Iron Age hillfort sits in the middle of an ancient woodland once known as Bishop's Wood, created as a deer park by the Bishop of Exeter during the thirteenth century. When the wood was taken over by the Forestry Commission, it was replanted with a coniferous cash crop but thankfully the fort was protected. You can still see the two silver stars at both entrances, which were erected to remind the Commission where they couldn't cut and replant. The hillfort has never been investigated archaeologically but one day its secrets may be revealed.

BUZZARDS FLYING OVERHEAD

40

REMAINS OF THE GUNPOWDER WORKS

GUNPOWDER STORES

3.   Having explored the hillfort, walk back up to the main trail and continue right. The views are lovely up here and the pine woods to the left of the path are lovely to wander in. The trail opens into a large clearing and then continues on. After a short while you reach a second clearing, not as obvious as the previous one.

4.   The large trail now peters out into a couple of smaller paths. If you want to cut down to the valley floor through the wood take the path to your right, if you want a slightly longer walk, take the path in front of you. This will head out of the woods and just as you reach a dip, turn right downhill, following the edge of the woods.

i Eucalyptus Trees: Planted in 1965 by the Forestry Commission, these are the remnants of a failed experiment, looking at eucalyptus as a cash crop.

i Gunpowder Works: Gunpowder was increasingly being used in the mining process but was a dangerous product to make. Gunpowder works were sited near rivers so that the powder could be kept damp and clothing washed down. Despite these precautions, explosions were a common occurrence. The Cornwall Blasting

5. You are now on the valley floor with the river running on your left. After half a mile keep an eye out to your left just after the river starts to split into several streams. Between the path and the river is a collection of abandoned buildings that were once part of a gunpowder works.

A few yards on, the path coming down from the hillfort, rejoins the path you are now on. As you continue walking you might spot a grove of large *eucalyptus trees* to your right. A bit further on by the river bed is another collection of building foundations also belonging to the gunpowder works.

6. Continue along the path until you return to your car park. As the path rises up, away from the river, this is your last chance to wash the dogs down before you get back to your car.

Powder Company began manufacturing gunpowder in Bishop's Wood in 1863. They moved into the buildings vacated by a former tin plant but sadly, it didn't get off to a good start following a "fearful explosion" in 1864 which killed and injured many factory girls. The works remained in operation but suffered from a shrinkage in business due to the contraction in the local mining industry, as well as a growing preference for dynamite. It was eventually broken up for scrap in 1887.

LINKS:

The Gunpowder Process This link takes you to information about the larger Kennal Vale Gunpowder works, in Cornwall. Page 3 onwards explains how gunpowder was made and the same steps would have been used here in Bishops Woods. https://bit.ly/2pYHUSc

PHOTO ALBUM:

https://flic.kr/s/aHskAkevns

7

ST CLEMENT'S RIVERSIDE

LENGTH: 3 miles
EFFORT: Easy
TERRAIN: Riverside path
FOOTWEAR: Trainers or boots
LIVESTOCK: None
PARKING: Limited parking is in a lay-by on the side of a private road. Park by the dog bin. The postcode will get you near but don't follow all the way up to the school. TR2 4BW
WCs: None
CAFÉ / PUB: None
OS MAP: 105
DOG BINS: At the car park and half way point

BRIEF DESCRIPTION: A short walk with no hills. This is a really lovely walk and is great for spotting wildfowl. Can be muddy after a high tide or heavy rain but perfect for dogs that want a less taxing stroll.

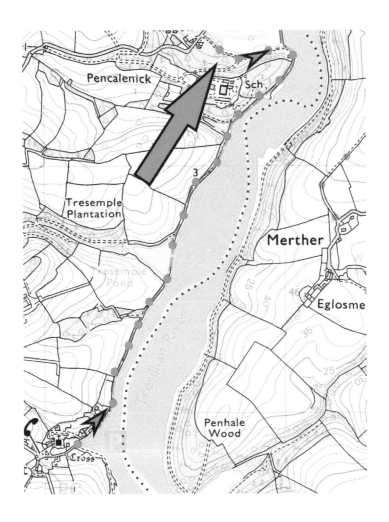

Elevation Profile

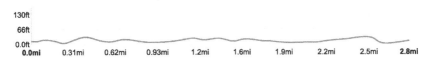

130ft									
66ft									
0.0ft									
0.0mi	0.31mi	0.62mi	0.93mi	1.2mi	1.6mi	1.9mi	2.2mi	2.5mi	**2.8mi**

TRESEMPLE POND

DIRECTIONS:

1. From the lay-by, walk forwards and leave the tarmacked road when it bends right uphill, heading down the unmade road. Follow this road down to the river and veer to the right. Walk past the large five-bar gate and continue on. The path will turn from unmade road to track, but remains wide and flat until St Clement. After heavy rain or a very *high tide*, the track can be quite muddy.

2. Shortly after the large gate, there is a small track leading down to the river. From here you can walk out onto the river bank and explore what looks to be an old boathouse.

Birdlife: Some of the birds that you may see whilst on the walk.

Cormorant: A very large black bird with a primaeval appearance. Although a seabird, this is a tidal river and you can often see the odd cormorant sunning itself on the mud flats, with its wings outstretched.

Curlew: A curlew is more often heard before it is seen. It is the UK's largest wading bird, with a very long curved beak, and a distinctive call that is loud and plaintiff.

3.   Returning to the track, it is just over a mile to St Clement. Halfway along you will pass a large lake on your right. This is a great spot to see *birds* during high tide. During low tide they are all over the mud flats, as well as on the lake. Keep your eyes peeled and see if you can also spot the occasional seal or two.

4.   As you get to the hamlet of St Clement, there is another five-bar gate. If you need a dog bin continue past the gate. You are asked to keep all dogs on leads as you take the path through the hamlet.

5.   From here retrace your footsteps back to your car. There is a small stream nearby to wash off muddy dogs.

Heron: An even larger bird, the grey heron can be spotted on the bank side or flying down the river like an ancient pterodactyl.

Little Egret: This is a relatively new bird to the British landscape, once it was just a summer visitor but now there are established breeding colonies all over England and most successfully in the South West. It is a small white heron and is often noticeable due to its bright white plumage.

CURLEW

LINKS:

RSPB Birds www.rspb.org.uk
Tide Timetables https://bit.ly/2IOJw9I

PHOTO ALBUM:

https://flic.kr/s/aHsmh5G57X

8

PONTS MILL

LENGTH: 3 miles
EFFORT: Moderate
TERRAIN: Good footpaths, can be muddy
FOOTWEAR: Trainers or boots
LIVESTOCK: None
PARKING: Ponts Mill car park at the end of a no through road. PL24 2RR
WCs: None
CAFÉ / PUB: None
OS MAP: 107
DOG BINS: None

BRIEF DESCRIPTION: A gorgeous woodland walk through a vanishing industrial landscape. Walk through the remnants of a tin and copper industry, that then moved into china clay back in the 1800s. To experience the modern china clay industry choose Walks 9 and 10. This walk offers great exercise for dogs as they rush up and down the hillsides.

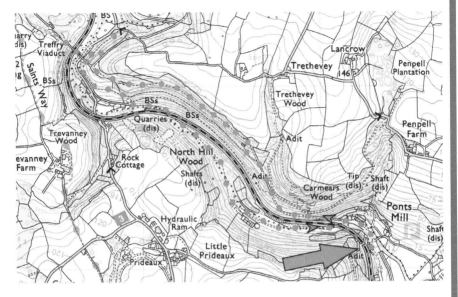

Elevation Profile

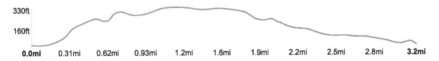

DIRECTIONS:

1. From the car park, with the river in front of you, turn left and walk upstream. Head towards the metal gates and walk through, passing the Luxulyan Valley notice board.

2. As the path veers left before the railway bridge, take the clear footpath on your right. Climb the few steps, go through a kissing gate and then start walking uphill. If you look down at the path you are walking on, you can see evidence of the *Carmears Inclined Plane* tramway. To the right of the path is a small stream and after heavy rain you can spot lots of small waterfalls in the hillside to your right. After a climb, you will come to a stone bridge, just before it on the left is a small path, take this and then follow it onto and over the bridge. Now turn left and continue uphill.

Carmears Inclined Plane: This was a 1 in 9 horse-drawn tramway, driven by horsepower and the giant waterwheel at the top of the slope; it was used to bring the granite and china clay down off the hillside. Remains of the granite setts can still be seen at your feet.

Leats: A leat is a small canal; a man-made waterway created to deliver water to a particular location. The first leat you cross is the Fowey Console Leat and was built to supply water to the copper mines at Penpillick Hill. After you climb up the steps next to the waterwheel, and onto the top path, the leat that runs along this path is the Carmears Leat which was built to drive the waterwheel.

LOVED BY ALL DOGS

CHIMNEY AT THE CLAY DRIES

3. As you reach the small stream (*leat*), you will need to walk left, upstream. It doesn't matter which side of the bank you choose to walk. Your path now joins several others, there are two right-hand paths take the lower of the two. The leat should now be on your right and, shortly, the remains of the *Wheelpit Mill* although the wheel itself is no longer present. Walk along the path until you get to a massive *granite boulder* on top of the leat. Having examined it return to the waterwheel and take the steps to the right of the wheel. I would recommend putting dogs back on leads for this section, it is well fenced off but the drop is considerable.

4. At the top of the wheel take the footpath left. Dogs can come off the lead again now. This is the highest path in the Luxulyan Valley but can be prone to mud. Possibly because of the current closure of the top leat.

5. You will pass a stone with a K on one side and a T on the other. This is a boundary stone marking the boundary between land owned by Robert Treffry and Nicholas Kendall, although everything that you see on this walk is created by Treffry.

i **Wheelpit Mill:** Originally built in 1841 the water from the Carmears Leat flowed over the top of the waterwheel and delivered the power to help the horses haul the wagons up the inclined plane. When the inclined plane was abandoned, two large grinding pans were employed to crush granite and extract the suspended china clay. This was transported, in a liquid form, down to the dries down by the valley floor.

GREAT FOR EVERYONE

6.   The path now comes out into a large open area and what appears to be a large stone wall. This is the top of the very impressive *Treffry Viaduct*, although at this angle you can't see it properly. Looking towards the viaduct, we will be turning right onto another path, however it is well worth walking along the viaduct and back before doing so.

Crossing the viaduct is magnificent, with incredible views. Within the viaduct itself runs another leat, occasionally there are gaps in the granite path where, if you peer through, you might be able to see water running. I would strongly recommend dogs on leads if you do walk along the viaduct , Harry once tried to jump up onto the wall. I nearly died. At the other side of the viaduct and to the left is another disused leat, this is the Charlestown Leat that was built by Charles Rashleigh in the 1790s, to provide water to his newly built harbour in Charlestown, almost four miles away. Once back onto this side of the viaduct turn left onto the path mentioned above.

HIDDEN BUILDINGS

i   **Granite Boulders:** Along this walk, you will have to navigate huge granite boulders and you can see how earlier engineers dealt with some of them. If you examine the giant boulder by the waterwheel pit you can see a run of holes all lined up; these would have been made with tools called feathers & wedges, to calve off segments of rock. On this boulder, you can also see where it was successfully split for the leat. The boulders at Luxulyan are so exceptionally large that one was used to carve a sarcophagus for the Duke of Wellington's tomb in St Paul's Cathedral in the 1850s.

7.   Follow this path, with the wall on your left and then go through the gap and down some steps. The path now runs down through a very picturesque beech wood towards the valley floor. It's easy to pretend you are in a fantasy film set, with giant granite boulders strewn across the floor. Cross a small footbridge over the leat and turn left on the footpath. The leat should now be on your left as you walk back toward the viaduct.

8.   Keep to this path until you reach a place where there is a field on either side of the path. Continue along the path until you get level with the end of the fields and then cross the stile on your right to enter that field. Head down to the bottom left corner, through a kissing gate and turn left onto the path.

9.   Follow this path down towards the river. It will now take you all the way back to the car park, occasionally crossing over the river and under railway lines. Just over halfway, there is a well-preserved *china clay dry* complete with its chimney.

10.   Continue along the path until you return to the start of the walk. There is a small stream just before the car park in which you can wash your dog.

 Treffry Viaduct: Built by Richard Treffry in 1839, this viaduct is an engineering masterpiece. It has 10 arches, spanning 200 metres and stands 27 metres tall. The viaduct had a dual purpose, it was built to provide a tramway across the valley, but also to provide power to the waterwheel. Within the viaduct runs the Carmears Leat. You can sometimes see the water flowing beneath your feet. It is a stunning piece of architecture and is now a scheduled monument.

China Clay Dry: It is cheaper and easier, due to the weight and fluidity of liquid, to dry the china clay as close to its extraction site as possible and so, in the past, dries were built alongside mining areas. China clay arrived in a suspended liquid form at the back of the dry; it was then spread over the coal-fired drying floor. The dry china clay was then shovelled forward to the linhay area and was taken away by cart, tram or lorry to the docks on St Austell Bay. This dry was called Trevanney Dry, it was built in 1920 and closed in 1965.

ABOVE THE TREE TOPS ON THE VIADUCT

LINKS:

Luxulyan Valley http://www.luxulyanvalley.co.uk/

PHOTO ALBUM:

https://flic.kr/s/aHsmaY4bVU

9
....

SKY TRAIL

LENGTH: 2.5 miles
EFFORT: Easy
TERRAIN: Well-drained footpath and cycle path
FOOTWEAR: Any
LIVESTOCK: None
PARKING: There is a small car park just beyond a new housing estate. PL25 5RY. A larger car park is available across the main A road and accessed via a footbridge (PL26 8TX)
WCs: None
CAFÉ / PUB: On the other side of the large roundabout is the pub, The Carclaze Arms
OS MAP: 107
DOG BINS: In the car park

BRIEF DESCRIPTION: A short walk with excellent views over the china clay mines. Great for dogs, although pay attention to cyclists. This walk can be combined with Walk 10, Baal Tip – Clay Trails.

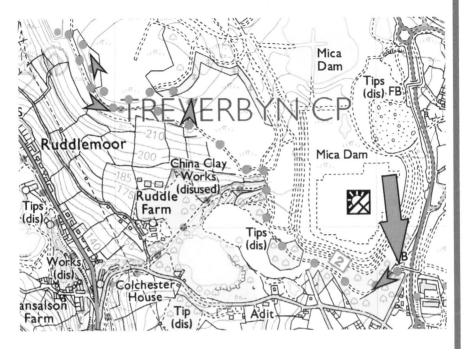

Elevation Profile

```
660ft
490ft
330ft
160ft
   0.0mi   0.31mi   0.62mi   0.93mi   1.2mi   1.6mi   1.9mi   2.2mi  2.4mi
```

DIRECTIONS:

Due to the close proximity of the A391 make sure your dog is on a lead when you get out of the car.

1. From the car park walk towards the footbridge and then turn left. You are now on National Cycle Trail, Route 2. It isn't a busy route but there will be cyclists especially in summer. Follow the path to the left and keep on it for about half a mile, at which point it has two left-hand turnings close to each other.

2. For a small diversion turn left at the second turning and head downhill. As the path turns left again, walk forward past two large granite boulders into the undergrowth. The slope now leads down to a small stream. This is a nice source of fresh water for dogs but it is also a nice example of two streams of two different colours converging, one is red from tin or iron, one is white from china clay. After heavy rain the difference is quite noticeable.

3. Return up to the main path and continue to walk forwards. The path, which begins to rise gently, is now part of the Sky Trail Spur and not part of Cycle Route 2. After a while you will see on your right a hut with a footpath leading off behind it.

i China Clay Industry: For centuries China dominated the porcelain industry, exporting it to Europe where it was in high demand as the local product, fine stoneware was an inferior product. In 1745 William Cookworthy was determined to locate a source of kaolin outside of China and found a deposit in Cornwall. He began to refine it and triggered an industry in Cornwall, and the St Austell area in particular that became a global market which has continued for the next two hundred and fifty years. It has shaped almost everything that you can see in this area of Cornwall.

ON TOP OF THE WORLD

RIDGE RUNNING

This following section is short and steep but gives amazing views over the surrounding countryside. Alternatively, you can continue along the main path as this smaller path will rejoin it later on.

4.   As the small path climbs it will turn to the left along a wire fence then open onto a plateau. From the summit, you can now walk along the spine of this clay tip. Looking down to your left you can see the sky trail spur. The landscape up here is littered with the remains of centuries of the *china clay industry*. Behind you is a giant grey triangular tip, to your left are small green pyramids. Collectively these were known as the *White Pyramids*. As

i **White Pyramids:** One of the most dramatic impacts the china clay industry has had has been on the skyline around St Austell. Looking around you can see lots of large pyramid structures, the largest of which is just above Carluddon. These are tips or slag heaps from the refining process. Once they were all white, earning them the nickname of the Cornish Alps now only the largest remains a whiteish grey, as the others have been terraformed and re-seeded.

you look down you can see incredible *turquoise coloured lakes* and as you walk along the spine, you can see the open-cast mining in the hillside ahead of you, across the valley. Carry along the spine, taking care as the path can be uneven and very windy, until the path gradually heads back down and rejoins the cycle path. As you come off the spine, if you look down into the valley below you can see *Wheal Martin, China Clay Museum.* If you want to visit for a greater exploration of the industry you will need to drive as there is no path down to it from here.

5.   Continue along the cycle path for about 400 yards at which point the path ends. Turn around and head back to the car by retracing your steps.

6.   If you wish to extend this walk, then once back at your car, cross over the footbridge turn left towards a car park and then follow the instructions for Walk 10.

Turquoise Lakes: Until you see these strange green lakes it's hard to appreciate how unusual they are. Ranging from milky blues to glowing emerald these lakes contain water rich in mica and copper mineral deposits, a residue from the washing of the clay. The water is perfectly safe, but swimming is forbidden. These are not naturally formed lakes; they are hollowed out pits meaning the sides are sheer, they are extremely deep and very cold.

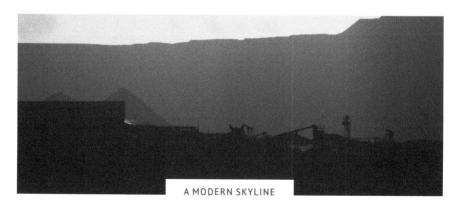

A MODERN SKYLINE

TURQUOISE LAKES

LINKS:

A Brief History of China Clay
https://www.cornwalls.co.uk/history/industrial/china_clay.htm
The Clay Trails http://www.claytrails.co.uk/
Wheal Martin, China Clay Museum https://www.wheal-martyn.com/

PHOTO ALBUM:

https://flic.kr/s/aHskxe3CiH

10

BAAL TIP – CLAY TRAILS

LENGTH: 3 miles
EFFORT: Easy
TERRAIN: Cycle and footpath
FOOTWEAR: Trainers. Some wet sections after heavy rain
LIVESTOCK: None
PARKING: PL26 8TX. This car park has been created by the closure of a road so old sat navs may get fooled trying to find it. You need to head to Carluddon and from the mini roundabout head down the No Through Road
WCs: None
CAFÉ / PUB: Closest pub The Carclaze
OS MAP: 107
DOG BINS: In the car park

BRIEF DESCRIPTION: An easy walk through a modern industrial landscape, there are lots of opportunities for dogs to wander free and explore. Walk through the remnants of a china clay mining industry whose alien landscape has been used as a location for Doctor Who. This walk can be combined with Walk 9, Sky Trail.

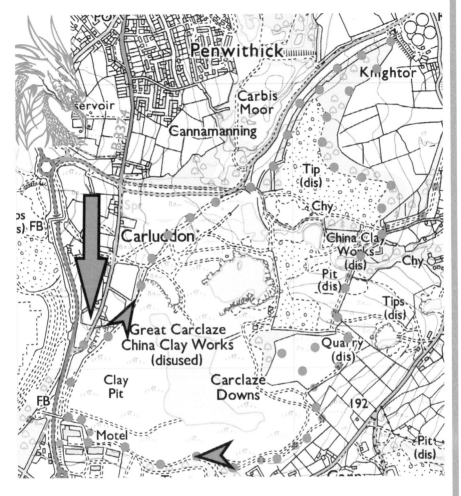

Elevation Profile

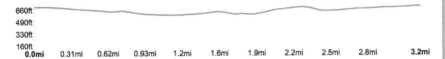

| 660ft |
| 490ft |
| 330ft |
| 160ft |

0.0mi 0.31mi 0.62mi 0.93mi 1.2mi 1.6mi 1.9mi 2.2mi 2.5mi 2.8mi 3.2mi

DIRECTIONS:

1. From the car park, with the pyramid behind you turn right and walk towards the road bridge, then turn left onto a lower unmade footpath and start walking left down the loose surface. Walk along the path with a large open cast mining pit to your right. Dogs are fine off the lead. The path beneath your feet is mostly made of mica, a by-product of the *china clay industry* as the majority of this walk is on reclaimed land. Go through the small wooden gate and continue forwards. Here the path comes to an obvious T-junction, turn left towards a waist-high wooden post and then turn right, and with the pyramid behind you, start walking down the path.

2. As you walk along this path keep an eye out for fence posts ahead. If you have an exuberant or "deaf" dog that doesn't like to walk to heal, then this would be a good moment to put them on their lead as the path moves towards the road and car park.

3. Head through the kissing gate at the fence posts and go straight across the wide path and onto a small footpath heading into the trees. This footpath runs alongside a road for this section. There is plenty of room to the right for your dog to explore but if you are not confident,

i **Modern China Clay Industry:** Cornwall is the third largest exporter of Kaolin (china clay) in the world and was once the leading exporter after China, before other global deposits were found. It is hydrologically mined, this means that high-pressure water cannons are shot at the rock face to extract the kaolin as a water-based slurry. The slurry is then taken off to the dries. China clay is a global industry and is used in a vast range of products, from medicine to coating paper. It is an industry that has literally changed the face of Cornwall bringing wealth and opportunities to an otherwise impoverished area.

TOWARDS THE PYRAMID

SUNSET AT THE STONE CIRCLE

keep them on a lead. Continue along this footpath for another half a mile, this section can be muddy after heavy rain but it's also a great spot for blackberries. As the path starts to rise put your dog on the lead as the path ends at another kissing gate by a car park and road.

4.   Go through this kissing gate and turn right, then walk through two large metal gates. Dogs are now fine off the lead for the rest of the walk. Follow the path through scrubland, ahead of you, you can see a ridge which you will soon be walking along.

5. When you get to the next set of gates, head through the far left set and walk towards the fence on your right. Start walking up the ridge alongside the fence, you are now walking on a massive spoil heap. The views up here are spectacular, behind you, in clear weather, you can see onto Bodmin Moor. Follow the fence on your right, all the way along until you come back off the heap. Ahead of you, you can see a wide white path which is your next route.

6. Continue down on the current path. As you leave the fence you now join National Cycle Trail, Route 2. Walk forwards and go through a metal gate, there is now a long hill in front of you, walk to the top. Turn left at the T-junction at the top, following the cycle trail and then just where the bushes end, turn right, leaving the cycle trail and take the steep grassy path up the hill. As you get to the spine of the hill turn right and carry on up until you reach the *stone circle* at the top. Walk through the stones towards the fence and have a look down at some of the pits.

Stone Circle: This is a modern stone circle that was built by English China Clay when they landscaped this hill. It's a nice thought that for whatever reason the Cornish are still building stone circles.

FIELDS OF FOXGLOVES

7. Now return through the stones, and as you pass the king stone, a large boulder on its own, turn right and take the grass path back down the hill overlooking St Austell Bay. At the bottom rejoin the cycle path and turn right. From here you will circumnavigate Baal Pit, ignore any left-hand turns. You can see why this location was used for a Doctor Who episode, Colony in Space. It's also worth considering that whilst it looks barren and alien, this is exactly what the *Eden Project* looked like before it was transformed. Walk past a shelter with some benches and continue along the path.

ENJOYING THE VIEW

8. As you approach a road bridge put your dog back on the lead. If you want to extend this walk climb the steps, cross the road via the bridge and follow the instructions for Walk 9. Otherwise, turn right and walk back to your car.

LINKS:

A Brief History of China Clay
https://www.cornwalls.co.uk/history/industrial/china_clay.htm
The Clay Trails http://www.claytrails.co.uk/
The Eden Project https://www.edenproject.com

PHOTO ALBUM:

https://flic.kr/s/aHsmaY1DEm

11

ST ANTHONY'S HEAD

LENGTH: 7 miles
EFFORT: Moderate
TERRAIN: Coast path
FOOTWEAR: Walking boots
LIVESTOCK: Cattle possible
PARKING: Porth National Trust car park. TR2 5EX
WCs: Towan Beach / St Anthony's Head
CAFÉ / PUB: Towan Beach – seasonal
OS MAP: 105
DOG BINS: A few along the way

BRIEF DESCRIPTION: A lovely walk around one of the Roseland's headlands taking in St Anthony's Lighthouse, Place House and St Anthony's Church, exploring the beautiful Cornish creeks and coast. Dogs are on leads for sections of this walk, and although there are often cattle, it is a really lovely walk and gives everyone a really good stretch. Two stiles, one easy, the other trickier but spaniels handle it fine.

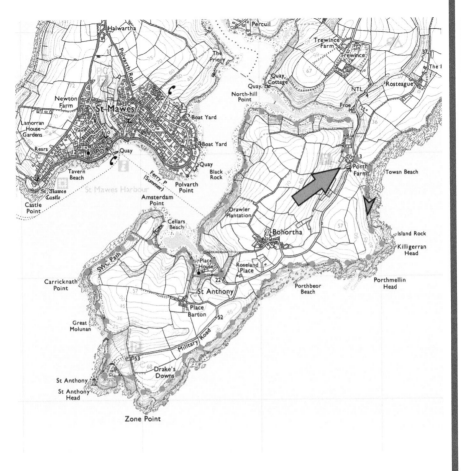

Elevation Profile

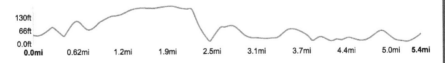

DIRECTIONS:

1. From the car park head down to the beach going through the cluster of National Trust buildings. When you get to the coast path turn right and walk to St Anthony's Head. This is a two-mile section with two stiles, a potential for cattle and some high cliffs. The advice is to keep dogs on a lead. This section of coastline is very scenic and if you are lucky, you should spot seals surfing in the waves.

2. After a mile and a half, the land to your right drops away and you can see over to Falmouth. Soon after that you will get to St Anthony's Head. Here the path appears to fork, take the left-hand path and looking down to your left you should see a bird hide in the cliffs below. The path now heads through a defensive wall and you will find yourself in *St Anthony Head Battery*. Have an explore and then make your way to the front of the residential single-story buildings.

3. The coast path continues to the left of the road in front of the residential properties. Follow the path with the metal handrail down the hillside. There is an option, halfway down, to turn left and visit the Battery Observation Post and the Bird Hide, the views from both these spots are excellent. Return to this point and continue down the steps. At the

St Anthony's Lighthouse: Fans of Fraggle Rock will recognise St Anthony's Lighthouse from the opening sequences. Whilst the lighthouse is now a holiday let, the light and fog horn are still operational but automated. This is an incredibly busy stretch of water as you can probably see for yourself, from traditional red-sailed Falmouth oyster boats to ocean going liners and super tankers. In the middle of the bay sits Black Rock and further down the coast lurk the Manacles, a low-lying collection of rocks responsible for hundreds of shipwrecks over the centuries. The lighthouse was built by the Admiralty in 1835, replacing previous beacon fires.

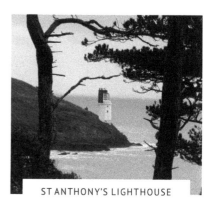

ST ANTHONY'S LIGHTHOUSE

TOWAN BEACH

end of the handrail, you can turn left to view *St Anthony's Lighthouse*, although it is private and can only be viewed from a distance. Otherwise turn right.

4.   Dogs are fine off the lead for the next section. Keep on the footpath until you see a collection of large pine trees ahead. This section is very scenic but the path gets close to the edge again, so best to have dogs back on leads. After you have cleared all the pines, the path now heads into fields and so long as these are clear of cattle, dogs will be fine off the lead. The views to your left overlook a large section of water called Carrick Roads, the large town opposite is Falmouth with *Pendennis Castle* to the

i **St Anthony-in-Roseland Church:** Nicolas Pevsner, in his catalogue of the finest buildings in the English counties, considered St Anthony to be the best example of a twelfth-century parish church, in Cornwall. Originally it was part of a larger Priory but that's long gone. There is a beautiful Norman door at the entrance and although it was modernised and restored in the nineteenth century much of the original building remains. One of the side doors leads directly into Place House a private residence that overlooks Cellars Beach.

left edge. As you walk along you will spot a twin castle on the edge of another land mass, this is *St Mawes Castle*.

5.   As you walk past a beach there is a wood ahead of you, the path heads uphill to a signed gate in the top corner of the field. You are now entering a conservation area so dogs will need to go back on the lead.

6.   Follow the path as it joins a private lane. The coast path now skirts behind *Place House* but the signage is very clear as the path leaves the lane. It now goes past *St Anthony-in-Roseland Church* which is a lovely place to visit and then continues out onto a small road where you turn left and head down to the water.

i **Place House:** Place was built in 1861 by Sir Thomas Spry in the style of a French chateau. He was also responsible for restoring St Anthony's Church and this was no doubt when the door to the church from the house was added. The church originally belonged to a Priory which has long gone. *Place Ferry* connected this remote section of the Roseland to the rest of the peninsula, estate workers from Falmouth and St Mawes would come across to work. As the estate wound down the ferry was abandoned until the establishment of the South West coast path when it was resurrected.

i **Pendennis Castle / St Mawes Castle:** These twin castles were built by Henry VIII to defend Carrick Roads from invasion. Whilst the cannon fire from one side wouldn't protect the whole entrance, twin fire covered the whole waterways. This was an important stretch of water both from the Channel and the Atlantic and was vulnerable to attack due to its size.

PLACE HOUSE

7. When you get to the water's edge follow the signpost to *Place Ferry*. The coast path now continues across the water via the Ferry but we continue along the footpath into the woods.

8. The next mile and a half is mostly in woodland so is safe to have your dogs off their leads. Keep the water on your left at all times and ignore any right-hand footpath signs to Borhotha. At the end of this section, you will come to a long wooden bridge over a stream and boggy area. There is a road on the other side of this bridge, so dogs back on leads. Once across the bridge turn right and head back to your car. There are two car parks near each other, if you didn't park in this one just walk up the road and the second car park is on your right.

ONE TRICKY STILE

LINKS:

The National Trust at Porth https://www.nationaltrust.org.uk/porth
St Anthony Head Battery
http://www.castlesfortsbattles.co.uk/south_west/st_anthony_head_battery.html

PHOTO ALBUM:

https://flic.kr/s/aHsm5enf9Q

CARDINHAM WOODS

Well loved by dog walkers, Cardinham Woods deserves a special mention in any dog walking book. There are a wide range of walks throughout the woods where the paths are always well-drained and not muddy. Most importantly there is an excellent café.

The only reason it's not officially included is that all the paths and routes are so well laid out there is no need for me to do it, other than tell you to visit!

EXTRA HELPINGS

KNOW YOUR TIDES

NB. All figures on this page are rough guidelines. Tides are vastly intricate and complicated, but this will hopefully prove to be a rough but helpful explanation.

The sea goes all the way out and then a bit later it comes all the way in again, and it does this twice a day, day in day out, forever. Whilst it might seem mystical, it works like clockwork and is easily understood, although there is a lot going on.

In the course of a 24-hour day, you will get four tides, two high and two low, each six hours apart. High, low, high, low, high, low and so on forever until the moon falls out of the sky. Within those six hours, a large volume of water is heading either in or out, and it's worth remembering how much power is involved in the sheer volume of water on the move.

Low tides are great for rock-pooling and big open beaches for cricket and frisbees, spreading out and goofing about. High tides are better for boat launches or swimming closer to the beaches edge, snorkelling over rock-pools, or paddling without having to walk ages to the water's edge.

When you arrive at a beach have a look at where the high tide line is. You can easily spot this; it will be a long line of seaweed, this shows how high the previous tide got. Place your towels above this line or be prepared to move them as the tide comes back in. Also consider where you park your car if there are signs saying that a road is liable to tidal flooding, no-one is pulling your leg, and never park on the beach.

The height of the tide is governed by the moon. When the moon is full or new, we get spring tides, when the moon is halfway between full or new, we get neap tides. So, within the course of a lunar month (28 days), we get two spring tides and two neap tides. Spring, Neap, Spring, Neap, Spring, Neap and so on until the world ends. Spring tides, therefore, have nothing to do with Spring, they happen all year round.

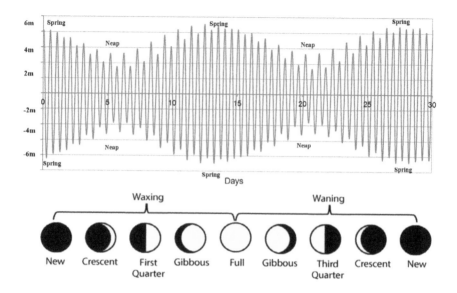

WHAT THIS ALL MEANS

Neap tides give low level high tides and high level low tides. Neaps are normal for want of a better word and provide a nice and easy tidal exchange, up and down, in and out, nothing too dramatic, nice and normal. There is still a large change in the height of water, and the volume of water moving around and still deserves respect and care, but it's nothing like what happens during the Springs.

Spring tides are responsible for high level high tides and low level low tides. Springs are super for all sorts of reasons. Firstly, a spring low tide means that the sea goes a long way out and reveals things not often seen, old wrecks, sunken forests etc., it also means you have access to coves that you normally can't walk to. It is essential that you know when the tide is turning to avoid getting either cut off in the cove or overtaken by an incoming tide. The RNLI picks up people every year left clinging to cliff faces as their fabulous uncovered cove disappears as the tide comes in. And remember it's a spring tide, so it's going to be extra high and extra fast.

A spring high tide is when the sea comes into its highest point, and this is generally when flooding occurs. Most times this is nothing more dramatic than the sea gently lapping into the streets around the harbour in Mevagissey or fully covering the beach at Caerhays. If at all.

In Cornwall, the tidal range difference can swing between 3 metres and 6 metres depending on springs and neaps.

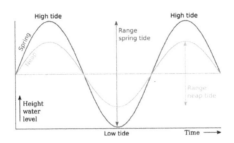

Major floodings tend to occur when you get a low-pressure system out at sea, (low-pressure gently allows the sea height to rise, a low of .960 allows the sea to rise by 50cm) a low-pressure system usually also brings wind and rain, the wind pushes the waves in and rain fills up the rivers giving the incoming spring high tide nowhere to go. At this point, there is just too much incoming water and it comes in further and higher than the beaches and harbours.

Finally, spring high tides happen around 12 am and pm and the lows around 6 am and pm. Neap high tides are around 6 am and pm, lows at 12 am and pm. Of course, these times apply to Cornwall and will vary in other parts of the world. As the moon moves between full and new and then tides move from neaps to spring the times will also move.

This may all seem confusing and complicated, but it runs like clockwork. If you stay in one location for 7 days, you can see the difference in how the tides behave for yourself. There's a lot more to all this, and if you are interested, there is lots of information on the internet, start with the Met Office or the Marine Coastal Agency.

So there you have it, easy and like clockwork. All you need to do is look at the moon. Alternatively, buy a tide timetable, all coastal communities sell them.

SEASONAL RECIPES

There's nothing nicer than foraging for your own supper. Here are some of my favourite, and easiest recipes, from the most obvious and abundant foods you can find whilst out walking.

SPRING – RAMSONS

Ramsons are a small leafy spring plant that flourish in woodlands. They are also known as wild garlic, and you can often smell them before you see them. The first thing to emerge are their green leaves, usually in huge swathes, followed later by a small white flower blooming above the leaves. They start appearing in February and March, and are generally gone by May. Their smell is very distinctive; if you pick the leaf and it doesn't smell strongly of garlic, then it isn't ramsons.

RECIPE: *Fry some bacon bits or diced chorizo in butter, as they get close to being fully cooked add the hand dived scallops. Give them a few minutes on each side. As you turn the scallops over, throw in a large clump of chopped ramson leaves. When the leaves have fully wilted, squeeze some lemon juice over and serve.*

SUMMER – MACKEREL

It's going to be tough to catch a mackerel whilst out walking but how can you talk about Cornish food and not mention mackerel?

RECIPE: *Chop your fillets into small chunks, dip them in a simple flour and fizzy water batter, shallow fry in oil, dip in sweet chilli sauce. Wonder if life gets better than this. Best served on a secluded beach over a campfire eating the fish you have just caught.*

Alternatively, bake the whole fish in foil and serve with gooseberry sauce.

AUTUMN – BLACKBERRIES

Beyond the obvious, eat as you walk and don't eat the ones below knee height (dog wee), there are loads of things to do with black-berries. They aren't as big or as sweet as the commercial ones, but a perfect sun-ripened blackberry is a total joy.

RECIPE: *Blackberry and apple crumble. If you are lucky enough to find a wild apple tree so much the better, otherwise grab a cooking apple. Chop and stew down with the blackberries, some cinnamon and a bit of sugar. Place in the bottom of an ovenproof dish. For the crumble weigh an equal amount of butter to flour and ground almonds combined, and sugar. Omit the almonds altogether if you want. Just make sure that the butter and dry ingredients are equal in weight, one third each. Rub them all together until you have a breadcrumb mixture. Spread over the top of the fruit and cook until the juices are oozing up through the crust. Serve with custard and joy.*

WINTER – SLOES

Sloes are a blue-black berry that grow on blackthorn bushes. They grow in abundance along many sections of the coast path in autumn and look like blueberries although they are a lot harder. The bushes are generally tall and form a hedgerow, sometimes above your head and very thorny. They are very sour but given time they taste delicious. Sometimes people recommend freezing the sloes for a night before use, but I've never tasted the difference.

RECIPE: *Get a bottle of gin or vodka and empty the contents into a jug. Fill the empty bottle with sloes, no more than half, add a few spoons of sugar and then fill up with the gin or vodka. Drink the remaining alcohol or make another load. Reseal the bottle. Put to one side, every couple of weeks, give it a small shake. Decant for Christmas and enjoy. This gets better with time so put a bottle to the back of the cupboard and rediscover it in a few years. Decant and consider how clever you are*

RECOMMENDED READING

Reading a story set in the place where you are staying / living, always adds an extra something. When the author describes a scene, you are instantly drawn further into the book. The following great stories are set in the area and benefit from that extra dimension.

Rebecca
Daphne du Maurier

The House on the Strand
Daphne du Maurier

Fault Line
Robert Goddard

Up with the Larks
Tessa Hainsworth

The Camomile Lawn
Mary Wesley

OS Map 105

OS Map 107

EXCERPTS FROM *SCRIBBLES FROM THE EDGE*

The following essays are from my book, *Scribbles from the Edge*. Scribbles is a collection of my weekly column for the *Cornish Guardian*. They are lifestyle and commentary pieces and the ones I have selected here focus on the fun and failures that go hand in hand with owning a dog. I hope that you enjoy them.

HARRY THE RUBBISH GUN DOG AND HIS RUBBISHER HANDLER!

As some of you may know, we have a springer spaniel going by the name of Harry. He's three years old now, and I have always meant to get him trained properly, it is after all what he is bred to do, and after my column on prevarication the other week I finally picked up the phone and spoke to a trainer. On the phone, Mel seemed very nice and we agreed to meet up and see if Harry was up to the grade. We met up at Minions and in reality, she seemed every bit as nice as she had on the phone but it soon became apparent that it would be a question of whether I was up to the grade just as much as Harry!

So Harry and I got out of the car and instantly my heart sank. All around us were wild ponies and sheep, I'm afraid Harry is pretty good but not perfect and I was concerned that things might career down the pan before we even got started. However, Mel agreed that they would be too distracting for him and we moved them on so that we could begin our work. At first, Mel wanted to know what I'd taught Harry, we'd obviously already failed the ignoring sheep test. I explained that we'd only really done the basics but that Harry was pretty good at those. It turned out that he wasn't. I demonstrated how well Harry walked to heel, Mel pointed out that Harry was walking to heel when he felt like it because he liked my company not because he had been told to. The minute something more interesting came up, say a gorse bush or a butterfly, he was off. His recall was equally suspect. Yes, he did come back to me but not always, once again that passing gorse bush could be an attractive thing to a dog with clouds in his head. The stay command worked well although I had been doing it wrong. Apparently, when you tell a dog to "stay" you must always return to him, you shouldn't call him to you because stay means just that. If I want him to sit in one spot and then come to me it's "Sit" and then "Come here". Or rather three blows on the whistle. Which I didn't have.

We then began to walk in circles and squares and figures of eight which I kept getting wrong, memories of my terrible attempts at dancing at Burn's Night earlier in the year came flooding back and Mel seemed quite bemused by someone that couldn't complete a figure of eight without getting lost. After that humiliation, we progressed onto retrieval work, which Harry thought was great fun and acquitted himself fairly well. At the end of the session, Mel thought that Harry had promise and I needed to do some home-work so we went away happy with our progress. So far, he's walking to heel on the lead perfectly and off the lead, he's pretty good except for the odd gorse bush. Sit and Stay are also working well but he seems to have nosed dived when it comes to retrieving. One thing at a time is going to have to be our motto. I'll let you know how we get on.

WALKS WITH HARRY

We've been having some really beautiful weather recently. I appreciate that having typed this, it will now start to rain and by the time you read this you will no doubt be up to your armpits in water and beginning to develop webbed feet. If this is the case then I apologise wholeheartedly. But for now, the good weather has meant that my walks with my constant companion, Harry, have been enjoyable expe-riences. Actually "constant" isn't a terribly good descriptive word for a companion who is by my side for about 10 seconds during the whole walk, but he does nip back now and then to check up on my laborious progress or to show me a rabbit that he has managed to catch, or even better a rabbit that someone else caught a week ago. Dogs do love a good strong smell and in his generosity, Harry assumes that I do too.

For this reason, my preferred walks with Harry don't end near a rabbit warren. Too many times I have made the mistake of not getting him back on the lead in time and then just waiting uselessly whilst my dog undergoes paroxysms of ecstasy as he dashes uselessly from one thicket to the next. I also like to end the walk near a source of running water, this means that he can have a drink and I can give him a quick scrub down because the thing that Harry loves almost as much as a good scent is a good mud pool. In fact, if he can find a stagnant bog then he is in heaven. It always amazes me how even in the most severe of droughts my "oh so " dog can find the last patch of dark, stinking mud available.

It is fun watching him play though, he'll go from walking to trotting, then a wee bit of a jog and suddenly he'll see a movement and he'll accelerate from a canter to a gallop to finally flying as he launches himself through the scrub and up and over obstacles with his back legs flicking out behind him. Despite these Nimrod like qualities he just about always fails and pads back to me, tongue lolling, having enjoyed the chase as much as any end goal.

Walks on the beach are just as much fun, all those wonderful seagulls which hang teasingly above his head. The other day he was so intent on launching himself at a flock of seagulls that he completely misjudged the depth of water beneath his pads and suddenly plunged into a deeper section and had to doggy paddle his way back to a shallower point. As I watched the seagulls laugh at him I thought about the best way to describe the shock on his face for this column, and to comment on how rather vacant in the brain department my dog is. Just as I was thinking this my foot plunged into a hidden dip on the icy cold seabed and water poured down the top of my boot. I don't know if I actually heard Harry snigger but his tongue was definitely lolling in an even more amused fashion than normal. As I sloshed back to the car I decided not to comment on the intelligence of anyone who fails to spot dips on the seabed.

ONE FOR THE BIRDS

This week seems to have been one for the birds. On Saturday, Harry and I went for our regular rugby stroll down to Polridmouth beach and along the cliffs when half way down I began to hear a shooting party coming from the Menabilly estate area. I wasn't that bothered as Harry is unaffected by loud bangs; fireworks don't faze him, two screaming boys don't faze him so why should some distant guns? As we got closer to the beach he hared off into the undergrowth and came back proud as punch carrying a dead pheasant. Nothing for it now but to head towards the guns and return one of their birds, it was so funny watching Harry trot past the Labradors and proudly drop his find at the feet of the shooters. It's a strange way to see birds up close when they've just been shot but I'm afraid I'm not sentimental about it, I eat them and they taste great.

Which is just as well because on Monday, Dave dropped in a brace of pheasants and partridges to the shop. Oh good, I thought as I eyed their splendid plumage, how the hell do I prepare a whole bird. In the end, I chickened out and just removed the breasts. I know it was a bit wasteful and I had some great casserole and roast recipes in front of me, but one of the birds still had grain in its gullet and it was all a bit too much. When I was younger I couldn't even enter a butcher's, because the smell of blood would make me very queasy but like most things you just learn to suck it up. Not the blood, that would just be gross, in fact, I'm making myself queasy again so I'll move on.

Having dealt with the birds I had to dash off to get the boys so I wrapped the four birds in newspaper, popped them in a bag and dashed off. It would be hard to describe the slaughterhouse scene that greeted me and the boys on my return. In a rare show of co-operation, the cats and Harry had got the bag off the table onto the floor and then opened it up. Blood, feathers and body parts lay all over the floor, table and chairs, three living animals looked very pleased with themselves and four dead ones looked even deader. My boys just stood there looking on in shock! Harry tried to look nonchalant but was unable to pull the look off properly as he had feathers sticking out of his ears, the cats just looked at me as if to say "and?"

Moving away from game triumphs and disasters I've also had a great week bird spotting. This is a perfect time for it as there are no leaves on the trees and branches and so the birds can't hide so easily. Obviously, bird spotting isn't so easy with Harry, I usually just see the backs of birds as they fly away in alarm but sometimes I get lucky. On Tuesday morning a walker told me to keep an eye out for a kingfisher, the man had seen it every day for the last week at this spot. I have to say I haven't seen it once! I have seen lots of others though, chaffinches, goldfinches, curlews, chiffchaffs, pipits, turnstones, stonechats and maybe a cirl bunting – this last one is unlikely as they're not supposed to be around here but it really didn't look like a yellow hammer which is the next closest thing it could have been. So there we go, if I haven't been massacring or inventing them I've been spotting or eating them. Hope you enjoy our feathered friends as much as I do.

CORNISH WALKS SERIES

Walking in the Mevagissey Area
978-0993218033 https://amzn.to/2FsEVXN

Walking in the Fowey Area
978-0993218040 https://amzn.to/2r6bDtL

Walking with Dogs between Truro and Fowey
978-0993218057 https://amzn.to/2jd83tm

MORE BY LIZ HURLEY

A HISTORY OF MEVAGISSEY
An engaging and informative history of Mevagissey.

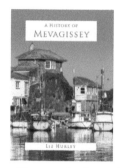

For over eight hundred years, Mevagissey has flourished beside the south Cornish coastline. It was, in its heyday, a globally significant port, lighting the streets of London in the eighteenth century and feeding the homes of Europe. It has been battered by freak storms and a cholera outbreak but has continued, unbroken, contributing in no small part to the colonisation of the world by Cornish men and women.

This potted history gives an insight into the history of the village and takes a humorous look behind the scenes, revealing what it is like to actually live and work in Cornwall's second largest fishing port. It debunks a few myths and introduces some lively, tall tales, as told through local voices.

Available in bookshops.
Paperback: 978-0993218026
Digital: https://amzn.to/2r5VlkA

SCRIBBLES FROM THE EDGE
When everyday life is anything but every day.

Liz Hurley gathers together her newspaper columns to deliver a collection of fast, funny reads. Join in as you share the highs and lows of a bookseller, dog lover and mother in Britain's finest county. This treasure trove of little gems moves from lifestyle pieces on living day-to-day behind the scenes in the UK's number one tourist destination, to opinion pieces on education, current affairs, science, politics and even religion. Watching the sun set over a glowing beach isn't quite so much fun when you are trying to find the keys your child hid in the sand, and the tide is coming in! Join in and discover just how hard it is to surf and look glamorous at the same time. Batten down the hatches as she lets off steam about exploding cars and rude visitors. Laugh along and agree or disagree with Liz's opinion pieces, as you discover that although life might not be greener on the other side, it's a lot of fun finding out.

Available in bookshops.
Paperback: 978-0993218002
Digital: https://amzn.to/2ji2UQZ

LOSING IT IN CORNWALL

The second collection of columns from Liz Hurley, still scribbling away on the edge. Still trying to hold it together. From serious to silly her columns cover all that life throws at us. A perfect selection of little titbits, to pick up and put down or read straight through.

Available in bookshops.
Paperback: 978-0993218019
Digital: https://amzn.to/2r4eHGG

HELLO AND THANK YOU

Getting to know my readers is really rewarding, I get to know more about you and enjoy your feedback; it only seems fair that you get something in return so if you sign up for my newsletter you will get various free downloads, depending on what I am currently working on, plus advance notice of new releases. I don't send out many newsletters, and I will never share your details. If this sounds good, click on the following: www.lizhurleyauthor.com

I'm also on all the regular social media platforms so look me up.

GET INVOLVED!

Join *Walkers Talk Back* on Facebook, to read about the next book in the walking series. Suggest routes, give feedback, receive advance copies. Better yet, share photos and feedback of the walks you enjoyed.
https://www.facebook.com/groups/841952742623247/

Did you enjoy this book? You can make a big difference.

Reviews are very powerful and can help me build my audience. Independent authors have a much closer relationship with their readers, and we survive and thrive with your help.

If you've enjoyed this book, then you can leave a review on Goodreads.

If you read it online leave a review on the site where you purchased it.

Thanks for helping.